Love to Live,

Live to Love

Bennie Foster

authorHOUSE®

AuthorHouse™
1663 Liberty Drive
Bloomington, IN 47403
www.authorhouse.com
Phone: 1 (800) 839-8640

Published by AuthorHouse 12/21/2018

ISBN: 978-1-5462-7286-1 (sc)
ISBN: 978-1-5462-7285-4 (e)

Print information available on the last page.

Any people depicted in stock imagery provided by Getty Images are models, and such images are being used for illustrative purposes only. Certain stock imagery © Getty Images.

This book is printed on acid-free paper.

About the Author

Born in Greenville, S.C. on Oct. 05 1954
Lived a good portion of my life in a small
Town called Greer... (near Dobson).

Then moved to another small town; Lyman S.C.
A small community called Fairmount,
My parents bought their first home.

My parents: Ben and Lillie foster,
I'm the oldest of five living sibling.
Three brothers and two sisters.
I'm married to a very special lady.

I attended Florence Chapel high until
Eight grade, then graduated from
Byrnes high, then started working,
A lot of different jobs as I moved
Through life.

I've seen and done a lot of things in my sixty
Four years of life. That's my experience...
With things I lived and loved in my journey
So far in life. I'm special to my Lord who
Gave me my talent of writing poetry.
He strengthens and guides me.

Contents

Godsend

I didn't know at the time, not a clue,
That God was sending me someone like you.
With a big heart, sweet smile and truly a blessing,
A unique personality that keeps you guessing.

I sometimes believe that you have a gift to feel,
When a person is in need and you set out to heal.
A good person with insight, you have the skills,
To help them overcome with the strength of your will.

A welcome pleasure, I think sent from above,
A star shining bright, a cup of love.
You're a Godsend, a messenger not from the sky,
But of the earth, doing special things til you die.

Knowing you has been my pleasure,
Sharing time with you is something I really treasure.
You're only one of the Godsend, I believe there's many,
I'm blessed to know one, some don't know any.

Many Blessings

When first we open our eyes...
Yawn and stretch our arms to the sky,
Before we smile and start dressing...
The Lord has given us our first blessing.

After glancing out the window, we make our bed
Have some breakfast or some fruit instead,
We wake the kids, get them started dressing,
Low and behold.. God has given us another blessing.

With health and strength we go about our day
Taking care of business, just going our merry way
We come home, unwind and start undressing,
Not even thinking, God has given us another blessing.

After eating and talking the day turns to night...
We prepare for sleep with hopes of another day in sight,
Taking the time while on our knees confessing,
We thank the Lord almighty for all His many blessing.

I'm Thankful

I'm thankful for my eyes, that I have sight,
While many have eyes, but have never seen the light.

I'm thankful for my legs, which help me to stand,
While others have legs, but need a helping hand.

I'm thankful for my brain, which allows me a choice,
Others have ideas, but still have no voice.

I'm thankful for my hands, that I may be able to hold,
Many have the reach, but struggle to gain control.

I'm thankful that I'm unique, one of a kind,
For what God gave me is truly all mine.

We Don't Try

Women and children are being abused,
Parents and loved ones are used.
It's a vicious cycle we can't deny,
We can't make it better if we don't try.

The police try to set a positive role,
Some use their power to be in control.
People do cruel and mean things we can't lie,
We can't make it better if we don't try.

Some politicians try to make our lives better, being leaders,
Others are lowdown, no better than bottom feeders.
Our government is so corrupt, it makes you want to cry,
Guess what we can't make it better if we don't try.

A Mother's Love

A mother's love is bold, direct and pure,
Something to hold on too, always sure.
No matter the problem... no matter the plight,
She will take charge of the situation, make it right

A mother's love is kind, pleasing and strong,
The kind of love you need when things go wrong,
God made her special with blessing from above,
There is no charge for her unchanging love.

A mother's love is willing, able and true,
Will give what you need to get you through.
Always good advice and a helping hand,
Providing you with what only a mother can.

A mother's love there from the time you are born
Guiding, protecting... as you come from her loins,
To you mom, and all mothers everywhere, I say,
Love and thank you... God bless you on mother's day.

Wake Up

Wake up ... open your eyes, it's a brand new day,
Thank the Lord for my life is what I will say.
I could have passed in the night you see,
And never knew all the plans He had in store for me.

Wake up ... take a deep breath, look around you twice,
See all the beautiful things, God has put in your life.
Now fall to your knees, bow your head and pray,
Thank you Lord, for letting me live another day.

Wake up ... go out into the world lift up your voice,
Tell how God gave His only Son to give you a choice.
Make a joyful noise, yes dance and shout,
Tell everybody you meet what you're so happy about.

Wake up... it's time for a change and do it now,
Pick up your bible, the word will show you how.
For God loves you, He said if you believe in me,
I will give you eternal life and your soul will be free.

The Man... (My Dad)

I try to imagine what you were like as a young man,
Would like to know so I can better understand
What makes you tick and where you get your drive,
Trying to be indifferent, but I can see the love inside.

Back in the day, I bet you were smooth,
Maybe a slick talker, probably had some dance moves
In a picture had on jeans, leg cuffs rolled up and a tight t-shirt,
Might have been a ladies man, cause I know you were a flirt.

The way you carried yourself, always with the tough vibes,
You were smart and had talent, lots of different emotions inside,
Did things your way, big kahuna... being tuff,
You'll take a few things but we knew when you had enough.

Dad you were great... didn't tell you, but you were the man to me,
Strong, very likeable and in the world for all to see
Now that I'm grown and finally got to know you,
I have no problem saying Dad I love you.

His Greatest Gift

He created the heavens, brought forth the light,
Moved mountains… gave the blind their sight.
Made the stars, made the waters run swift,
When our souls where in peril gave us His greatest gift.

When our minds are troubled, burdened and hearts ache,
Problems all around, just another we can't take.
We're weak and alone about to fall off a cliff,
Our souls are lost, gave us His greatest gift.

The world is in turmoil, the enemy is within,
All in a war… constantly battling sin.
Satan is driving, trying to give everyone a lift,
Our souls in trouble gave us His greatest gift.

Our redeemer, the saviour and the giver of life,
His only son he gave didn't think twice.
Bow your heads and call his holy name, He will lift,
Have faith in our Lord, he gave to us His greatest gift……

September Eleventh

As I lay in my bed, asleep...the world at peace,
I awaken, shaken... because harmony has ceased.
Thinking this day would be as yesterday, the same,
Only to find terror, a city in flames.

In horror, shocked in disbelief, watching the T V.
A part of me cries out...that could have been me.
People running, smoke rising, I stifle a scream,
Asking God.. why? and who would do such a thing.

Taking for granted at home that we're safe,
Then I wonder if there is such a place.
You never know when some madman will go astray,
And change the course of history in a single day.

Now we must unite, face this tragedy hand in hand,
Show what we're made of as only America can.
Our prayers goes out... God help us to be strong,
Make our justice swift, as we right this wrong.

For all of you suffering... it's not in vain
God will send his mercy and ease your pain.
God bless America our home sweet home,
As long as we stand together we're never be alone.

Best of Times

Friends getting together, talking over old times,
Reliving all the memories, while they are fresh in our minds.
Trips out of town, parties and cookouts are the ties that bind,
These moments in our history are the best of times.

Taking the kids to the movies, then out to eat,
Laughing and playing with them was such a treat.
Love them and enjoy the moment, because you'll find,
This memory was one of the best of times.

Getting together for the holidays, and reunions are so much fun,
Spending time talking with family is a way to bond.
The hugging and kissing and screaming, shouting, you don't mind,
Because sharing these moments, are the best of times.

Being alone at home or on the road are times I treasure,
It's peaceful and I reflect on them, it gives me pleasure.
All the little things that mean so much are just a sign,
That we must hold on to all of our... best of times.

All Lives Matter

My God made every living thing from the beginning to the end,
All lives matter, not just one...but every race of men.
Made us from the dirt, gave us life and we must serve,
All lives matter to him, He gave more than we deserve.

It's hard for me to believe that some think they're better than others,
We come from the same place, just different mothers.
I'm no better than you, and we're not more than them,
We serve one God, and all the glory goes to Him.

Stop. . . look at your neighbors, different but all the same,
We have similar stories, trouble in our lives, but who's the blame.
We're all human, trying to do right and not have our lives shattered.
God is good to us all, because all lives matter.

In this walk of life, on this path, we have but one goal,
To live holy, love one another and pray for our very souls.
We are in danger, destruction all around and lives being shattered,
We need to open our mouth and thank God that all lives matter.

He promised to love and keep us, my God does not lie,
Nothing in our lives will change, if we do not try.
We must give up our selfish ways, to keep our lives from being shattered,
People, fall to your knees and praise God, that all lives matter.

The long and short of it my sisters and brothers... stop!
And remember that God said we are to love one another.
I came to give you more of life, and not shatter,
Listen my beloved you are equal, and all lives matter.

I'm Waiting...

I'm waiting for world peace, let's end all wars,
Praying for a healthy tomorrow to heal all scars.
Looking for the answers to the questions, let's meet,
We can't find the solutions, if we don't seek.

If you're looking for a love to call your own,
Dependable, trustworthy...feelings that are strong.
Looking for a clue, try searching inside your heart,
You won't find the solution, if you don't start.

I'm waiting for the joy that I know is mine,
I'm relying on faith it will help me find.
Looking for the answers I kneel and pray
I know the solution... it's the only way.

Christmas is About...

Christmas is about a child born, given to us,
To bring a new life... a saviour to trust.
Jesus to take all our worries and even our fears,
To bear all our burdens and dry our tears.

Christmas is about being thankful for Gods son,
To give our all and let His will be done.
Now let us all gather both near and far,
Join hands, kneel and pray...look to the eastern star.

Christmas is about serving and giving to those who need,
To those who are hungry and those who don't believe.
Give to the homeless and the hopeless...a helping hand,
A place to live and a cause to make a stand.

Christmas is about Gods family and His enduring love,
Truth and honesty, mercy and all the goodness from above.
Search our hearts... pray and give Him our all,
For He will certainly pick us up when we fall.

Christmas is about the greatest gift of all time,
Given to us in love to save all mankind.
In no store can you find, at any price,
The savior of man... the giver of life.

AMEN

Imagine...

Imagine...living in a world with no hate,
A world filled with love, now wouldn't that be great.
Working hand in hand everyone getting along,
Building a better future and making our world strong.

Imagine...A world so full of love with all people willing,
To do whatever it takes to help stop the killing.
Where our children can live, learn and continue to grow,
Let's take off the false faces and let our real feelings show.

Imagine...A world with no wars, only peace...
Settling our differences with words, the fighting could cease.
As we strive to conquer hunger and disease,
Concentrate on trust and faith ; down with poverty and greed.

Imagine...Now the world we really live in,
Hating, killing each other and living in sin.
Just imagine if we gave our life to the Lord above,
We could all know the meaning of peace and love.

I See You

I see someone strong and independent,
Someone full of life, also very intelligent.
I see someone who won't let just anything do.
Oh yes. . . I see you.

I see someone of character, can't be played cheap,
Someone full of spirit a person so deep.
Someone with charm, has a heart that's true,
Oh yes. . . I see you.

I see someone with a strong will, but can take,
What life will give, and won't break.
Someone who's funny also sometimes blue,
Oh yes. . .I see you.

I see someone's who is helpful, makes a good friend,
Who gives advice, hangs to the very end,
If you don't know, you better get a clue,
Make no mistake my friend. . .I see you.

Dedicated to myself...

Inspire

Inspire...to be the very best that you can,
Never start anything in life without a plan.
Be true to yourself, whenever you start,
Don't give in when you reach the hard part.

Inspire...someone you love to give their all,
Do what's necessary, be prepared for the call.
Anything worth doing will be hard, but give it a try,
Fight… keep going even if it makes you cry.

Inspire...Yourself to take control of your life,
If you fail once get up and try it twice.
You'll never get ahead if you don't begin,
Listen... you can't always lose, sometimes you win.

Can We Keep the Feeling

Can we discover new ways of finding contentment,
And different ways of handling our resentment.
I know there's a better way to find,
Total happiness, with love and peace of mind.

Can we deal with being bound in chains,
Finding a way to keep from going insane.
Our life will be a struggle, no end in sight,
But if we talk... we can make it right.

Can we keep the same love we had from the start,
And give it new life from deep within our heart.
Life can be rough, just like the weather,
With honesty and hard work we can keep it together.

Can we keep this feeling that's deep in our heart,
And never let jealousy come in and break us apart.
Keep this feeling always and forever,
Because I won't stop loving you... no never.

More Than Once

More than once I've hung my head and cried,
After things didn't work, no matter how hard I tried.
More than once I thought about giving up without a fight,
Then I'd pull myself together and try to make it right.

More than once life has pushed me down to the ground,
But I made up my mind not to be knocked around.
More than once I've had my back against the wall,
Problems all around me, I just refuse to fall.

More than once I've heard my mother's voice,
Saying… make a stand you have a choice.
In my day I've heard my dad say,
Keep on living son, tomorrow is a brand new day.

More than once God has blessed me with good health,
Gave me a loving family that means more than wealth.
More than once I've had a smile on my face,
Thankful for the things that can't be replaced.

Tis the Reason

Our Lord is good and there is no doubt,
He will provide and work all things out.
The Lord in his wisdom, His only son to give,
Gave His only begotten son so that we might live.

Tis the reason and there is no guessing,
Jesus is alive and the Lord gives His blessing.
So let us celebrate this day in every way,
With the king of kings on His birthday.

Tis the reason and it's Gods will,
Gave the gift of life, His blood was spilled.
Peace and mercy with a whole lot of joy,
To every man, woman, girl and boy.

Tis the Season

Tis the season... lo and behold,
When miracles happen and mysteries unfold.
You see the joy in everyone's eyes,
And parents everywhere are on the spy.

Tis the season to see and believe...
For all the right reasons we can achieve.
All the goals and meet all the needs,
For happiness that we as a people can perceive.

Tis the season to give and get...
All the wonderful gifts, we won't forget.
But most important and a top the list,
To give to those who don't have a special wish.

Tis the season to rise above,
Petty hatred and misery to give love.
Praise the man who makes the season...
Born this day to give it reason.

Without Grace...

Without your grace...
I would be lost in space,
A man with no place.

Without your grace...
I would have no taste,
A man with no face.

Without your grace...
I'd be a hopeless case,
A man with no race.

Without your grace...
I would lose control,
A man with no soul.

Without your grace...
I couldn't be a winner,
Just a man who is a sinner.

My Prayer

Oh LORD, Who is my God...
I come to you on bended knees
With my head bowed and my eyes closed,
Asking for your mercy... please hear my plea.

I come to You a humble man,
Asking for knowledge to understand
Wanting the wisdom only You can give,
For a better world in which to live.

God... in this land that You rule,
Things are out of control, men are so cruel.
We've forgotten what is right and things are wild,
Your people are wandering around in hopelessness like a child.

Oh Lord... take our hand and lead us on,
Take malice from our hearts and make us strong
You have the power to create the light,
Please turn us around help us do right.

Precious Father grant me one last plea,
Lead, guide and watch over my family...
Then when at last our time here is done,
I ask for a home in Your kingdom with Your Son.

Praise and Thank Him

Praise Him in the morning when I wake,
Thanked Him for every breath I take.

Praise Him for watching over me as I slept,
Thanked Him this morning as I took my first step.

Praised Him for another wonderful day,
Thanked Him as I went on to let God have his way.

Praised Him through the power of prayer,
Thanked Him for His love, that reaches everywhere.

Praise God for giving His only son,
Thank Jesus for my life, and let His will be done.

Sharing

Sharing everything the good and the bad,
Things that make us both happy and sad
Those events seem like moments lost in time,
Called memories that last and stay in our mind.

Sharing the joys of family and our loving home,
Together in love, separated, but never really alone
Enduring those times just reliving the past,
Makes life more pleasurable, because they last.

Sharing together the pain of a loved one lost,
Using each other's strength to get by at all cost
As we cross over the bridge in which all life begins,
We will cross that very same bridge as all life will end.

Sharing a bond of love for which none can compare,
Faith so strong, feeling so deep these we share
We let the glow of our love shine so bright,
That others lost along the way can see our light.

Hugs

It's been a rough day, nothing going your way,
Nothing going as it should, you'd give up if you could.
Well just take a second don't pull the plug,
Because all you really need is a hug.

Your body is in pain and aches like it's going to rain,
The kids are screaming and you're going insane.
Well... take a second to get out of the hole you've dug,
Give yourself a break, because all you need is a hug.

The headache you have won't cease, can't find any peace.
Stuck in midday traffic in a car you leased.
Well take a second and gather your thoughts, take a sip from your mug,
Breathe in the moment and hang in there you just need a hug.

No matter how hectic your life can get,
With all the problems and issues… don't fret.
Take a minute and reflect, I'm blessed, don't bug,
Because what you're going through can be helped with a hug.

Y'all Can't

Y'all can't come in here no sir,
Best you go, before y'all cause a stir.
You best scat now get on home,
Fore your ma and pa are all alone.

Y'all can't do this, ain't no joke,
No way, no how we gonna let you vote.
Best get your tails on down the road,
Fore the Lord Jesus be collectin' your soul.

Y'all can't ride up front best you get to the back,
These here seats for whites, not you blacks.
Best know your place fore you get whup down,
Cause y'all mess with us your body won't be found.

Y'all can't eat in here this fir white folks only,
Better find your own, or your folks will be lonely.
Y'all no better than think you'd got rights,
No way you get freedom, not without a fight.

Y'all can't believe white folks is gonna hold us down,
We'd be free now... we are standin' our ground.
You all can't beat us no more, cause you know who we be,
We are not colored any more, we are black and we are free!!

Back in the Day

Back in the day, when the Indians owned the land,
Peace and freedom was taken by the white man.
Came in great numbers with greed on their mind,
The red man would lose all even lives in a matter of time.

The white man spilt blood, took everything they ravaged,
Killed women and children, but they called Indians savages.
With no fore thought...they took all the land,
Started a war that would destroy the red man.

Didn't care, no thoughts of what was right,
The ground ran red with blood, spilt by the whites.
With sheer force they came and destroyed a race,
Put them on a reservation and spit in their face.

Back in the day...when it was all said and done,
The red man was controlled by a whip or a gun.
Back in the day, the laws were created by the whites,
It was all in their hands, whether it was wrong or right.

Lockdown...

I look out my window, I can't see far,
Want to leave can't get past the bar
I'm troubled, my mind is stressed no doubt,
In lockdown on the inside looking out.

I stand and watch as my life passes by,
Desperately wanting to run, but can only cry
My mind rushes back to the good times of the past,
I ask myself... how long will this lockdown last.

Every time I move my shackles hold me back,
Soul is tormented, chained to the fact
It's not love, but bondage that holds the key,
Trapped and lockdown... will I ever be free.

I know freedom tastes good, I want my share,
Don't want much from life, just someone to care
No longer will I stand by and be chained, and bound,
I will have my life back... I won't be held on lockdown.

Just Because I'm Black

Just because I'm black and very proud to be,
Means... I carry myself with respect for the world to see.
I'll stand for what I believe and only take what I've earned,
Try and give back to my people to show what I learned.

Just because I'm black doesn't mean that I'm a fool,
May not have a degree, but I won't be used as a tool.
I'm smart enough to know just what it takes to make it,
In this fast moving world where so many people fake it.

Just because I'm black I'll be put to the test,
To see if I can hold my own with the rest.
Yes I may fall down, but I'll get back up on my feet,
Hold my head up high, and smile at everyone I meet.

Just because I'm black... I'm not always treated the same,
People try to hold me down, I won't fall for that stupid game.
I'm strong, smart and black, this is what I expect,
To be treated as an equal, I've earned my respect.

Special People

(Dedicated to nurses, doctors etc.)

Thank you for being there in our time of need,
Sharing our pain and helping us to believe.
That with your skills and Gods good grace,
There are no problems we can't face.

I know your job is difficult and tough,
And things do get hectic and rough.
Through it all you still punch the clock,
Passionately during your duty, solid as a rock.

Thank you again for choosing your field,
To work with weak and help cure the ill.
So in our prayers to God we will ask,
Father give them strength to complete the task.

My God...

My God... why in this world, is there so much pain that I see,
My people don't know His word, so you can't believe
Living your life as though you have everything in hand,
But I tell you if you don't know Christ... you don't have a plan.

My God.. why are there so many people who have nothing to eat,
Why are so many of His children living in the street
It hurts my heart when I hear that a child died in a car,
Their loved ones say.. they will be okay, I'm not going far.

My God.. why are there innocent people locked in a cage
They lose their minds killing each other in road rage.
I hate to turn on the tv, always news that breaks my heart
Senseless and needless abuse tearing each other apart.

Why God.. why are we not helping one another to live a better life,
We're not concern, some turn their backs, and don't think twice
People are not safe in the places that they were born,
In their own land… they are lost and abused, their lives torn.

My God we're living in the last days and that's a fact,
If we don't turn to You, we'll never get on track
We are lost because we stop giving You the praise you deserve,
We need to fall on our knees, grab the bible and read the word.

My God .. I don't want to lose my soul and live eternity in hell,
I want salvation and joy, listen everyone to the story I tell
Time is short get right with the Lord, open up your hearts... pray
Please believe in Jesus... he died for us, He made a way.

Thank You Lord

Thank you Lord for waking me up today,
As I get on with my day, I'll let You have your way
Still in my right mind, I kneel and pray...
Keep me safe and humble in everything I do and say.

Thank you, Lord that I'm able to see,
All the goodness and mercy in what You do for me
Your love fills me and your angels show You care,
I will have no fear because you are always there.

Thank You, Lord for letting me rise and speak,
And for the clothes on my back, the shoes on my feet
Because of you, all things are possible and You are able,
To make everything right and put food on the table.

Heaven and Peace on Earth

A newborn... being born on earth,
This is heaven on earth.

A baby sleeping safe and secure in a crib,
This is peace on earth.

Children playing together unaware of race,
This is heaven and peace on earth.

Neighbors working and helping each other,
This is peace on earth.

People working together in time of distress, and death,
This is heaven on earth.

Nations walking hand in hand with love in their hearts,
This is heaven and peace on earth.

Never Know

We live each day, and plan for tomorrow,
When tragedy happens, we are left with our sorrow
Grieving.. we say I can't believe, yet we go on as before,
Living our lives in darkness, because we never know.

We take life for granted and live without fear,
Thinking we live forever, but death is so near
Things happen in this world that will make you cry,
As surely as you live, remember you will surely die.

Consider this fact and know that it is true,
As those around you pass, one day it will be you
So get your house in order and let your light shine,
Let the works you do give you peace of mind.

Who Knows...

Who knows what to say...
When a loved one passes away.
Who knows what to do...
To give strength and comfort to you.

Who knows about the anger inside,
The one who can dry the tears in your eyes.
Who can show you the way...
To make it through another day.

Who knows just what you're feeling,
The one who's able and willing.
Who's always there in your time of need,
All you have to do is have faith and believe.

Who knows more about a loved one lost,
Then the one who's son died on the cross.
Jesus is the one who can ease all your pain,
And all you have to do is call His name.

I See

I see so many changes in people today,
Doing whatever to whomever, just to get their way.
It's a shame the jealousy and hate in their faces,
Also the hurt and loss of lives in different places.

I see so much misery, the ruining of lives,
Homeless and confused as tears flow from their eyes,
Going through life, routinely. .not even a clue,
Of the disappointment, they are going to go through.

I see a nation torn apart, politician who are willing,
Not enough love to stop the senseless killing.
Men and women serving this country giving their best,
Seeing horrors that give them a lot of stress.

I see in us, a strong sense of self,
Our friends in trouble, we offer our help.
In times of disaster we unite as one,
Working side by side to get the job done.

I see that there is still hope in our lifetime,
If we hold together, pray for all mankind.
Divided we struggled, united we will stand,
One Nation under God, Together. . yes we can.

Spring Time

Flowers bloom, and pollen looms
Leaves return, and the sun burns
Lazy ways and pretty days
Birds appear, the children cheer
Start of reruns and lots of fun
Blue skies and fourth of July
Plow the fields and cook on the grill
Skinny dip and vacation trips
Rise at dawn to mow the lawn
Staying cool hit the pool
For goodness sake it's spring break, that's fine
The best time is springtime.

Chances Are...

Chances are that through this walk of life,
You will rarely see the same face twice.
If you do just what is the chance,
The two of you enter into a romance.

Chances are some things in life happen for a reason,
Like the sun rising and the changing of the season.
Noticing someone from across the room,
Your heart flutters, and your hope blooms.

Chances are this person is someone you'd like to know,
Take some time to develop a bond, watch it grow.
Sexy eyes, the flash of a smile, trembling you start to melt,
Life is a risk, but this is something you're never felt.

Chances are you might have never met,
Now with these memories, you'll never forget.
Today I think... fate put me in that place,
So I have to smile whenever I see your face.

Forget About...

Forget about yesterday, it's gone...
Concentrate on today let our love grow strong.
Don't think of the past and what went wrong,
Just hold on to the now and go on.

Forget about things that you can't control,
It will depress you, and destroy your soul.
Let love warm you and take you out of the cold,
Squeeze me and let passion be our goal.

Forget about your problems for they matter not,
This world can only hope to contain a love so hot.
Forever is not long enough for me to love you,
Just give yourself to me, I promise to be true.

Emotions

Look deep within my eyes and see what's there,
Search out my soul openly, feel that I care.

Touch your lips to mine know my desire,
Let us embrace the moment, quench the fire.

Time is short, and precious, let's not take it slow,
Come and run with these emotions, see where they go.

Now don't worry that these feelings may soon end,
We became lovers… but we first became friends.

Always and Forever

Always stand up for what you believe,
Always give what you can to people in need.
Always be there for your family and keep them first,
Always try to give your all even when you're at your worst.
Always be open and willing to learn,
Always show compassion and be concerned.
Always take life one day at a time,
Always let peace constantly be on your mind.

AND

Forever be humble, but keep your spirits high,
Forever stay true and be willing to try.
Forever go on loving everyone the same,
Forever keep striving to stay in the game.
Forever take the time to smell the flowers,
Forever pray for the ones who hold the powers.
Forever believe in God and hold to His hands,
Forever stay on course as you travel this land.

Proven and True

I've been around the block a time or two, but I'm no pro,
No amount of experience can say how a love will go.
Just let me tell you this and believe it's nothing new,
You need to put your faith in a love that's proven and true.

Broken promises, and rocky marriages I've seen it all,
When lies and doubts come after I do, you're headed for a fall.
Just let me tell you when there is no one else to turn too,
Call me up and try a love that's proven and true.

Take you out for dinner and a show, promise you the world,
Carry you home to mom and dad, this is my girl.
Just let me tell if the trips become far and few,
Let me hook you up with a love that's proven and true.

I'm not perfect, but you should get to know my heart,
Walk with me, talk with me and let this be a start.
I've got a good sense of humor and I won't leave you blue,
I'm a man whose love has been proven and true.

Move Me and Soothe Me

Feel the pain inside of me,
Touch it with love and heal me.
Do the things that move me,
Say the words that soothe me.

In my heart it's you that I desire,
Kiss me, hold me and quench the fire.
Do the things that move me,
Say the words that soothe me.

When I'm close to you my love, I can't hide,
Even far away from you I feel your vibes.
Do the things that move me,
Say the words that soothe me.

I'm a whole person with you, there is no denying,
I'm a better person without trying.
Do the things that move me,
Say the words that soothe me.

Hey Baby...

Hey baby, what's up I just called to say...
That I woke up this morning missing you today.
I think about you while I'm cleaning up my place,
Can't help but love you, cause you put a smile on my face.

Hey baby, I had a rough time last night,
Told you about it, now things will be alright.
When things are going bad, I discuss them with you,
Together we figure out what we need to do.

Hey baby, I know how I want my day to begin,
Call you up to hear your voice, let you make me grin.
Who could have known that day when we met by chance,
That our coming together would turn into a romance.

Hey baby, there's no doubt in my mind,
You're one fine person, and one of a kind.
Just wanted you to know that I'm a helpless case,
Every time I think of you a smile comes across my face.

Mr. Loverman

I saw you out in the park, it was around noon,
You were sitting on a bench eating ice cream, licking the spoon.
I noticed your body and my mind started to hatch a plan,
My insides churned, I knew it was a job for Mr. Loverman.

All smooth I strutted up to you and said with my sexy smile,
You look like you're having a nice day, mind if I sit with you awhile.
Slowly she looked me up from head to toe, motion with her hand,
I sit close our bodies touched and bam! she wanted Mr. Loverman.

It was magic the way we connected, I knew we would get it on,
I went back to my room and dressed, called her on the phone.
Met her for dinner and drinks, she was so hot! we walked hand in hand,
Dancing slowly she was melting, she was ready for Mr. Loverman.

I asked if she was comfortable, she said mmm… let me think,
As she started to undress, I fixed us another drink.
She sat on the bed and I caught a sight, I could hardly stand,
As we crawled under the sheets it was time for Mr. Loverman.

Months go by, we see each other every now and then,
To rekindle the fire and let our love come down again.
It's been so good she's hatching her on plan,
Making a move to hold on to Mr. Loverman.

Meet Me Halfway

In this life you must take a chance,
That things will work out... even a romance.
When you meet you hope love is here to stay,
You have to invest your time and meet halfway.

To keep a fire burning you have to add some wood,
It's the same with love, just do the things you should.
Build a foundation of trust, which is to say,
You have to do the right thing and meet halfway.

On this journey, if you seek out love,
It must come from inside, as well as from above.
There is only one way a love will stay,
You give it your all and meet halfway.

Now there is one thing, you must do and know,
You just can't talk about it actions have to show.
That your feeling are true and you're here to stay,
Because in everything, you're willing to meet halfway.

Physical Relationship

From the moment we met I wanted to explore,
Knew it would be physical when I enter the door.
I just had to have you, there was no doubt,
Satisfying each other is what a physical relationship is about.

We made plans to meet and get a room,
Would be a joining of bodies real soon.
We hit it off things were hot and without hesitation,
No meeting of the minds, just a physical confrontation.

The more time we spent, the stronger our desire,
Couldn't control our passion, it burnt like a fire.
We got along great and had good conversation,
Even had bad times, but intense physical copulation.

As time went by, we slowly grew apart,
Because it was mostly a physical thing from the start.
You must become friends first, in any partnership,
Or all you will have is a physical relationship.

Things Change

In a romance you hope feeling stay the same,
But as the years go by...things change.
No matter how much you try or what you say,
What was good last year, just isn't today.

Doing a fight, cruel words are exchanged,
You try to take them back... but things change.
Then you make up and try to go on,
Now surely some of the magic is gone.

The tension grows you call each other names,
You can't see eye to eye... because things change.
Relationship gets worse, now you don't even try,
Because now you're at the point where you just get by.

A beautiful union gone bad, it's a shame,
You promised to stay together... but things change.
Now you must regroup and find happier days,
Searching elsewhere... you both go separate ways.

If You Stay...

Things will be better I'm sure without a doubt,
As everyone wonders what I'm so happy about
Laying out on the deck at night watching the stars,
In the glow of the moonlight, talk about our favorite cars.

If you stay. . .
There will be fewer nights alone in my big old empty bed,
In each others arms we lay close no words need to be said
No holding back we let our love and our emotions flow,
Clinging in the togetherness... where lovers often go.

If you stay. . .
I can't promise that tomorrow will be a better day,
But I can do whatever is in my power to keep trouble at bay
God can give you shelter from the darkness of this world,
And I will provide love and happiness for my girl.

Give Me More Time

It was a sunny day when I walked in the place,
Had something on my mind, then I saw your face.
Don't know what it was, I had this feeling inside,
Something came over me when I looked into your eyes.

Got to give me more time to work things out,
Give me some space, so there won't be any doubt.
I said we need more time, we have to be sure,
That when and if we get together, our love will endure.

I seduced you with my charm and trapped you with my smile,
So you gave me your number and said call me after while.
You invited me to your home, you walked me in,
We had so much fun, I didn't want it to end.

After we spent some time, I had to be on my way,
Kissed you and hugged, we promise to meet another day.
I can't remember when I've had a better time,
So until we meet again... you'll be on my mind.

As Time Goes By...

As time goes by, nothing stands still,
Hurricane winds destroy everything at will.
People growing older day after day,
Children rebelling to get their way.

As time goes by death takes another soul,
While a new disease begins to take control.
Kids killing each other for no reason at all,
You can't tell the winter from the fall.

As time goes by reality has a new face...
War rages on threating to destroy another race.
We now have computers running the world,
Controlling the fate of every man, woman, boy and girl.

As time goes by our fate is at hand...
We've got to be strong and come up with a plan.
Be united, say enough is enough and make stand,
Take back our lives, as only we the people can.

Illusion

The world today is in a state of confusion,
People believe in material things, this is only an illusion.
A false idea can lead to things that are unreal,
We have faith in only what we can see and feel.

So many people can be misled... they easily trust,
Groups and individuals who are corrupt with lust.
These people control with power and greed, they create confusion,
Getting the people to follow blindly into a state of illusion.

A person's dream is to find the right situation,
To live their lives with great expectation.
Life's beauty and desires are the web of illusion,
That entraps their soul and mind with confusion.

A stranger approaches a child with a gift to confuse,
Planting in their young minds untruths to intrude.
With the lure of a prize, they create confusion,
They take our children, who are tricked by the illusion.

Believe with your heart and see with open eyes,
Don't fall for the illusions that many people try.
There are so many of us wanting to believe...
In the magic of life, but illusions make us naive.

Love Is...

Love is waking to a bright sunny day,
In your right mind... ready to find a way.
To reach out and help one poor soul,
Whose life is spinning out of control.

Love is taking a long ride to see the sights,
Walking the trails, seeing the birds in flight.
Seeing mother nature alive at her best,
It gives you the feeling of being blessed.

Love is seeing the look on a child face,
Light up when they visit a new place.
Experiencing new things for the very first time,
Something that will be forever planted in their young mind.

Love is a dream that comes true,
It will open doors for you.
Love is your face in the mirror,
With eyes that now see clearer.

A Love Letter

You have touched my soul, now my love knows no bounds,
Upon hearing your lovely voice, my feet float off the ground.
Looking into your eyes stirs a passion down in my soul,
Once we kiss, our lips touch... my life spins out of control.
With each passing thought my mind is forever on you,
Thinking of the sexy way you talk and the things that you do.
If you need me for anything, I won't give it a second thought,
Because the pleasure you've given me can't be bought.
Your good heart and loving smile lights up the room,
To light the path of love like rays from the moon.
You see good in every situation and that's a plus,
For building a lasting relationship this is a must.
You're a Godly person, with lots of love to give,
Just knowing you gives me purpose to live.
Not one minute, not even a second goes by,
That I don't feel you, I don't even have to try.
God made you for just this purpose... to make life better,
And I hope I've made my feeling known in this love letter.

All Alone

I awake all alone in my bed...
Feeling rush through me, messing with my head.
This ache is a pain that I feel inside,
From being alone and it brings tears to my eyes.

All day... and all alone, memories come flooding back,
The tightness in my chest, feels like a heart attack.
Day dreaming of special moments, I hear your voice,
We could have been together, but you made the choice.

As the day ends and turns into night...
I made the decision... and I pray that it's right.
Time will heal the wound in my heart,
And I know tomorrow will give me a new start.

My Mother

Strong, determine, and consistent... this describe my mother,
And her love of life teaches her children to love one another.
Honest, loving and kindness... I can only tell you what I know,
With her faith in family, helps all of us to grow.

Sweet, caring and giving... is how she lived her life,
She'd give everything and more to help someone and not think twice.
Faithful, precious and blessed... living by the word of God everyday,
Teaching, showing and guiding her family the right way.

You are loved and you are cherished...
Your children have come to say,
Thank you God, and mom...
Happy Mother's Day!

Me

I can only guess that I was a bundle of joy,
Born to my parents a bouncing baby boy.
Coming into this strange world and new place,
Where some people were judged by color and race.

I was raised in a home full of love,
Where my folks had to work hard to stay above.
With the need to survive and a strong will,
My parents taught me it was important to learn a skill.

Childhood was good... I didn't have it too tough,
Though I did have days when things got really rough.
With school in the morning and evening chores,
Chopping wood, and working in the garden, left my hands sore.

As I grew older and became more aware,
Of things in the world and how little some people cared.
I vowed to make a difference, take another view,
With the way I lived and in everything I would do.

Kids

Thinking back to the times long ago,
Things we did and now we do no more.
We tap the memories in our minds,
As we journey back... back in time.

As kids we used to run and play,
Doing crazy stuff, like playing in the woods all day.
We didn't have many toys, but we didn't' care,
Just made do with what we had and learn to share

As kids we learn to work and how to give,
A helping hand so we all might live.
A happy healthy life, and try to enjoy the best,
Our parents taught us to accept nothing less.

Mom and dad raised us up in the church,
Taught us the meaning of life and hard work.
As kids we learned an important fact,
To love one another and watch each others back.

Children Are...

Children are a blessing from God, this is true,
Who they are and what they become is up to you.
Teach them with a firm hand and guide them with love,
Tell them about the facts of life and the Lord above.

Be understanding with your kids, help them to learn,
To care for everyone and always be concern.
Show them your light, so it may lead the way,
To how they are supposed to live life everyday.

Children are the lifeline to our very soul,
They carry on after us so our story can be told.
Be proud of them and cherish them with every breath you take,
Love them, don't forsake them when they make a mistake.

Family...

Some people are lucky, they have a lot,
Others are fortunate with what they've got.
We can't take for granted we will always be here,
So we need to keep our families near.

Take the time to call once and a while,
To say I love you and bring a smile.
Make some time to get together,
Do it now, we can't plan on forever.

Make every effort to stay in touch,
The little things we do mean so much.
Tell the truth... how much trouble will it be,
To make time for our loved ones, yes... family.

Dad...

---◄◯►---

Dad, when I look at you here's what I see...
A man, strong and caring, devoted to his family.
Every step of the way, you put food on the table,
Provided for our wants, mostly needs because God made you able.

About being a father... from you I learned,
Be flexible and firm, in life only take what you earned.
Work hard, be honest and deal head on with life,
There'll be many times when you have to sacrifice.

Thinking back, growing up I don't remember a lot,
But more than often in hard times you gave as good as you got.
Now as time passed and I became a man,
We've grown closer and there is more that I understand.

Dad, you are the man that cared for his wife and kids,
I love you and I'm proud of all you did.
Thank you for being there and just let me say...
God bless you and keep you this Father's Day.

Thanks for Giving

Today we are gather together here to celebrate,
This occasion when we cook and bake.
Good food for eating and give praise for living,
For our good health, we say thanks for giving.

First let's give thanks to the Lord above,
For His mercy, grace and strength, His love.
Because of Him we can share these feeling,
And for His blessing, we say thanks for giving.

Now we've all made it through another year,
And it hasn't been easy, we've shed some tears.
So keep your head up and continue living,
By His amazing grace, we say thanks for giving.

Let's enjoy this food and remember these times,
With love, be thankful for the pleasures you find.
Now go with God and always be willing,
To live for today my friends and say thanks for the giving.

A Love Lost

As I look to the heavens the clouds roll in,
I feel in my heart a storm about to begin.
The light leaves and darkness takes it place,
I look for cover... the comforts of a dry space.

Slowly the rain begins to fall...
I'm in a corner with my back against the wall.
Watching the rain as it splashes against the pane,
Bringing back the memories that cause me pain.

A pain that only comes from a love one gone,
You think of the times when you were all alone.
You shared the good times and the bad,
Now all alone you feel so sad.

Sitting just listening to the rain,
A comfort comes over me, helping to ease the pain.
Knowing I had a chance to have your heart,
Something I'll carry to my grave... one small part.

My Brothers

As I sit here thinking of my father and mother,
I want to say thank you for my sisters and brothers.
Traveling down memory lane is a trip like none other,
Let me tell you the story of my loving brothers.

Growing up together we sometimes slept four to one bed,
Feet in faces, two at the bottom and two at the head.
We'd wake up in the morning after chores we'd play all day,
Wasn't a lot to do for fun, but we would find a way.

Out back we had a big shade tree, where we made dirt roads,
Down below our house was a creek where we go catch toads.
In the summertime we would take a special hike,
Fix a snack, go catch bees in a jar and be back before night.

After going to church, we would get our bikes,
And ride all over town, cruisin' taking in the sights.
We still share the memories every time we meet,
Just hanging with my brothers is always a treat.

Sharing a special bond with love, that is without a doubt,
Having brothers like mine is what family is all about.

Reach Out and Touch

Reach out... save the children from a world gone mad,
Touch them with kindness, try and stay away from the bad.
Give them hope where it was only despair,
Reach out with loving hands that show we care.

Reach out ... give the children of this nation more choices,
Touch them with purpose, listen... hear their voices.
Listen to their problems, let's help them find a way,
So they can reach their potential and live to see another day.

Reach out... give the children love and more of your time,
Touch them with patience, let them use their minds.
Watch them grow to be all they can be,
To help make the world a better place for you and me.

Reach out ... touch all the places where you live,
Fight to stop the violence, with the love you give.
Let's unite as all the people of the world should,
To give our children a chance at something good.

Hurt

It hurt so much when you walked out the door,
I knew there was a chance I'd never see you anymore.
As the tears began to flow, I felt my heart break,
I would have held on if I knew what was at stake.

Remembering all the times that you saw me flirt,
Never did I consider how it made you hurt.
I was foolish and made lots of mistakes,
I would have held on if knew the stakes.

Every time you came to me just wanting to talk,
I'd have an excuse, and just got up and walk.
Now I can't get another chance, it's way too late,
I could have held on tighter, if I knew I was making a mistake.

Your eyes and smile are forever gone from my sight,
I can only look at your picture and cry late at night.
Knowing what I lost now, it's something only time can heal,
The lost of your love and the misery I now feel.

Far From Home...

(Dedicated to our men and women in the military)

In a distant land far from home,
Away from your families, but not alone.
Far from the place you live, in a foreign land,
Serving your country, making a stand.

Doing your duty having made the choice,
To serve and protect, to give others a voice.
Far from home just giving your all,
Never hesitating to answer the call.

Far from your family, this time of the year,
We wish you good health and lots of cheer.
Know it's not the same being away from home,
You are in our prayers and you are not alone.

Far from home at Christmas time,
You're in our hearts and in our mind.
We sing your praises, and sing them loud,
You are our hero's...you make us proud.

Far from home, but in our hearts, we feel you near,
God has your backs so try not to fear.
Far from home your loved ones never out of your mind,
We are wishing you good cheer at this x-mas time.

Over the Hill

Over the hill... opportunity is just ahead,
You must pay attention to what is being said.
If you don't, you'll miss your ride needless to say,
It's one more thing being put off until another day.

Over the hill... just coming into view,
Are all the good things that can happen to you.
Stay the course continue to always believe,
That whatever you want to do you can achieve.

Over the hill... keep your goals in sight,
Don't give up on your dreams without a fight.
Anything worth having means paying the price,
Of course there are the benefits that make it so nice.

Over the hill... once your dreams come true,
People will sit up and take notice of you.
Be proud, be an example and let your light shine,
To show the path to success for others to find.

I Can Fly

I went through the doors of a place I barely knew,
To go on an adventure I thought I'd never do.
As I headed past the counter to board the plane,
I had to stop myself and ask am I insane.

As I walked through the isle I was met with a smile,
Take a seat, you'll be with us for a while.
With the ring of a bell came the captains voice...
Thanks for flying delta and making us your choice.

So I sat in my seat not knowing what to expect,
While the stewardess got everything in check.
With a roar of the engines we took to the sky,
I glance out my window and saw I could fly.

I could never imagine the sight as I sit there,
Flying above the clouds, floating on air.
It felt good and strange at the same time,
Being this close to heaven gave me peace of mind.

The clouds looked like land covered with snow,
So majestic, beautiful and time seem so slow.
Never have I experienced or been so high,
As I soared through the sky... I knew I could fly.

You

I'm so happy that you are in my life,
To keep you there I wouldn't think twice.
I'll do whatever it takes, this you'll see...
Because I want to keep you here with me.

If there is something you want, just relax,
I'll get it for you, I've got your back.
If there is something you need just believe,
I'll make it happen, yes indeed.

With your sexy ways and mystic grin,
The things you make me want to do should be a sin.
I take in your views and talkative ways,
I could go on listening to you for days.

When first we met I didn't even realize,
That your wit and charm would have me so surprised.
I was amazed at every little thing that you did,
Just your presence around me, gave me the joy of a kid.

Old Blue

(Views on Growing Old)

Each day I thank God for letting me wake,
But I'll be darn, if I don't have a brand new ache.
Yesterday it was my back, today it's my shoulder,
Man... I sure love this life, I just hate getting older.

I remember in my twenties, I could see like a hawk,
A few years later I need these blame glasses I bought.
Hey I use to party and stayed in the streets,
Now I need two aspirins and seven hours of sleep.

Back in the day I wore an afro and was tall,
Look at me now, I've shrunk and gone bald.
Use to play basketball all day, have plenty energy left,
Now when I walk from room to room, I'm out of breath.

Well I know I've got to grow old... there is nothing left,
Keep on complaining I ain't ready for death.
Yes I've got my health, so let the story be told,
There are a lot of aches and pain to growing old.

Old Blue

(Views on being Broke)

When you don't have any money, just plain broke,
Can't do nothing, can't go anywhere, hey it ain't no joke.
A simple fact, no money, and you can't get a loan,
You can always find these folks at home.

You've got a job and you work every day,
But you can't get ahead, because of all the bills you pay.
You can't get overtime, so... what can you do,
Just scratching your head, feeling down and blue.

Just sitting around worried, you want to believe,
That if I have a little faith and some luck I can achieve.
When the bank calls wanting a payment on the note,
They don't want to hear excuses, don't care if you're broke.

Running to those loan places getting nickels and dimes,
That's not the solution, you just getting farther behind.
Asking your friends and family for cash, may ease your mind,
It's only a temporary fix, it may buy you a little time.

There's no quick remedy, people...you can only pray,
That a change in your luck is on the way.
Just believe me, you're not the only one who's broke,
Take it from somebody who's been there, I know it ain't no joke.

Old Blue

(Views on Drama)

The rent is due, but you don't have it all to pay,
You call the landlord and think of something to say.
He's heard all the excuses, well… what can you do,
If you don't have his money, hey the drama's on you.

The bank is calling, the car note is due,
Spent most of the cash on other bills, what's a man to do.
Racking your brain, just leaves you feeling blue,
If you don't have the cash, the drama is on you.

Work is over, time to rest and drink,
Feel like doing nothing, but that's what you think,
Your girl says… you don't take me nowhere,
You used to love me (drama) now you just don't care.

The relationship is over, now you're on your own,
Yeah it's rough making a new start all alone.
Paying support, picking up the kids and dealing with their mother,
So come on face the drama, if it ain't one thing… it's another.

Old Blue

(Views on Money)

Money can open doors and make dreams come true,
With enough of it, there's almost nothing you can't do.
If you take a few dollars, you can buy a house,
With enough money you can even get yourself a spouse.

You've got to have a good job to get paid,
Even need a few dollars if you want to get laid,
Must have the money or you won't get far,
Those with money, believe they are better than you are.

You can't live comfortable without the cash,
You won't make it long in retirement without a stash.
To get the money, it's best that you work and earn it,
Yet! there are the few that are bold and crazy enough to try and take it.

Some have it easy, and they know how to make a buck,
Some work hard at it and never have any luck.
Make no mistake, money does make the world go round,
If you make enough of it... you're the big dog in town.

Old Blue

(Views on high Gas Prices)

Well people I know that you know the time has arrived,
The blame gas prices are so high we can't afford to drive.
It's been a long time in coming, but we didn't know,
When it was going to happen or how high it would go.

It was once under a dollar, the good ole days are gone,
Now it's over three, almost four how I cry and moan.
Used to take under thirty five to fill my car,
Well... now it's over fifty and it doesn't go far.

What can we do us poor folks about the price of gas,
Nothing but whine and talk a lot of trash.
Those with Hondas and Nissans shake their heads when they see,
Us at the gas pumps, trying to fill our suvs.

To all you fatheads who control the price,
Hope something happens to you and hope it's nothing nice,
Oh and you Mr. President who don't have to worry about the price of gas,
Hope your legs grow together, and we all find out about your past.

Printed in the United States
By Bookmasters